A FAIR PLAY 1001 EDITION

In buying this book, you are giving two pounds to cricket initiatives for kids and teens around the world. In selling one thousand books and more we hope to sponsor kids and teens to play cricket, help them with their cricketing skills, and along the way give them opportunities that will serve them in life as well as cricket.

Pass it on,

Lance and Beef.

The Sandpaper Affair

Ten Naughty Cricket Stories

And One Extra Long On(e)

M.T. Sands

M.T. Sands grew up in southern England. She has been following cricket, and particularly the England team, ever since the day she ran away from school in disgrace and hid in the boy's pavilion. Over the years she has been unable to resist the lure of white and the joy of the Wormsley Oval. She hopes that you will also find equal joy in these pages of cricket tale and excess under the firm guard of her editors, Messrs. White and Wargh.

"Cricket is not a game. It is war by other means. Bring on the Ashes, mate!"

Steve 'Lance' Wargh, Bondi Beach, Australia

Riposte:

"Cricket may be a war, but the Ashes is always a bloodbath for the touring team."

Luke 'Beef' White, Hambledon, Hampshire, England

WHY READ THIS BOOK

Me and my Pommie mate, Beef wanted to say a few words about cricket. First off, even if you do not know anything about cricket, we think you should read this book because it tells you about life. To coin a phrase cricket is about life, and life is exactly like the cricket, innit. Secondly, Mary Sands writes like she plays cricket. She has all the best shots. She can hit you for six, or stroke you for four. Not only does she write funnily and well about the cricket, but she gives it all a wicked spin of her own. Finally, there is something magic about a cricket field whether it is a dusty strip in the African veldt, an Indian gulley or Jamaican Beach, the finest lawns of Melbourne or the lovingly trimmed squares of the English shires. We hope these stories will tell something about the magic and the love so many of us feel for this special game.

GO WELL,

Lance and Beef

Contents

The WomanKad

My earliest memories of cricket take me back to when I was at school. Unusually for a girls' school we had a cricket team. One of the girls' fathers, known to us as Roopey, had been a county player. Roopey was our sponsor and also our coach. Most of the time we played other local girls' teams, and sometimes, if we were lucky, the boys' under fifteens. But such was Roopey's enthusiasm that he would get us fixtures with touring teams. We all loved Roopey, and Roopey loved us, though not as people might insinuate today. He was a jolly good coach and thoroughly

1

decent man. - I also played rounders, but I much preferred cricket. Because of Roopey and the aforementioned opportunity to meet boys...

Everyone was excited, I recall... The Bangalore Pashmeekers were on their traditional early season tour of the home counties. Their reputation proceeded them, especially that of the Puri Sisters: Anika, Anima and Anita. We had played them the year before, and we had gone down to spectacular defeat. Anita bowled us out; Anima took the catches behind the stumps, and Anika batted us off the park. Now the girls wanted revenge – none more so than our Captain Hazel Flint, or Flinty as we called her.

I almost didn't play. A couple of days before I had twisted my ankle, whilst attempting to climb a gate in a pair of heels. The things we do for a snog at seventeen!

The Pashmeekers were batting, and as in the previous year, Anika Puri was taking us to the cleaners. They were 111 for two, and Anika was well on her way to fifty – having taken Flinty for a couple of classy fours, one through the covers and the other a delicious on drive that bisected me and Mousey, who was, I should mention, my best friend but not the best of fielders.

Flinty and the girls were desperate for a breakthrough. "How desperate?" I asked at the change of overs.

"Listen," said Flinty, "I don't bloody want to lose to this lot again. They were insufferable last time."

"Don't worry," I said. "There's something I can do, but it's a bit manky."

Flinty looked at me with alarm.

"It isn't cheating?"

"No," I said, "it's perfectly legal. Roopey told me."

I set up to bowl my dibbly dobblies as I thought of them to myself. Anika was backing up rather keenly at the crease. As she was about to set off for a run, I did a pirouette and removed the bails with the ball in my hand.

"Howzat?"

The Indian master (and Roopey's friend naturally) looked at me and said:

"Are you sure you want to do that?"

"Oh, yes," I said and looked around at the girls who were all stunned into silence.

The Indian master put up his finger:

"Sorry, Anika. You're out."

"But she hasn't even bowled the ball."

"Anika," the Indian master said, "you must accept the Umpire's decision."

"But it's cheating."

"I'm sorry to say it's within the laws, if not the spirit of the game."

I looked around at the girls, but no one was celebrating.

The following over Flinty took me off, and I was sent down to cow corner for the rest of the innings.

The Pashmeekers continued to pile up the runs. Anima, who had come in after Anika, made a very nice forty. Their final score of 170, however, was not insurmountable. In the break between innings we heard that Anika Puri was still inconsolable – sobbing into her batting gloves.

No one was talking to me – all except Mousey, of course.

"What are you going to do? – Flinty says you should be off the team."

4

"I've made a right Horlicks of everything, haven't I?" I said, all ready to burst into tears myself.

As it happened, the opportunity arose to make amends. Our innings got off to an inauspicious start – two wickets down, but Mousey who batted at two was a sticker. And that day she stuck. Together with Flinty she took us past the hundred. When Mousy was out for a very good forty, I realised that we were probably going to win.

We were six down, and Flinty was at the crease when I came out to bat. We needed thirty runs for victory, and I was determined I should not be party to it.

Flinty was batting as she normally did – with calm authority – and those crisp clips and neat tucks off her skirts. It always amazed me how it never rose up and remained forever pressed to her lovely thighs. Meanwhile, I was swishing and swiping at the ball as if I had forgotten how to hold a bat, or had mistaken it for a Rounders stick.

Flinty was obliged to come down the pitch. "Get a grip on it," she muttered between gritted teeth.

The next ball I swished or swiped as before. The ball popped up and went bouncing off into the covers.

"Yes" I screamed, charging towards Flinty. For, in case you have not guessed it, I was determined to run myself out.

But at the other end, Flinty was ball watching. When she turned and saw me screeching and haring toward her, she had no time to react.

Flinty slipped, and her skirt rose up to reveal a pair of sensibly white Marks and Sparks knickers. Humiliation!

And it was all my fault.

I had run out Flinty and mankaded[1] a Puri Sister.

Furthermore, I had been sent to Coventry by the entire upper and lower sixth.

Could things get much worse?

A few days later, everyone found out that I had also snogged Flinty's boyfriend. It was for this reason that I decided to run away from school.

That, however, is another story.

---

[1] So called after Vinoo Mankad ran out Bill Brown in this way during Australia's 1947 tour of India. – Lance.

The Flooring of Henry

"I'd never bet on something like that," said Fast Johnny adamantly.

"You did."

"I didn't."

"You did."

"This is getting childish. Anyway, I don't remember it."

"Be that as it may, I bet you can't reach the boundary edge before that limping, three-legged Yorkshire terrier. It's your ball."

"Are you casting aspersions on my fitness?"

"It's nothing to do with fitness, Fast. You still owe me."

"I owe you nothing. It was an honourable bet."

"And what could be more honourable than coughing up when you owe us? Come on, mate. That ball really is yours."

"Alright, Henry, keep your hair on. I'm after it."

Henry was playing for the French House one balmy Sunday on Parliament Hill. The Constant Gardeners were batting, and things, as usual for the French Boys, were looking pretty ominous. The Constant's opener, Barley Reed who would rarely offer a shot other than to prod or dab a single, was beginning to time the ball with a certain agricultural sweetness. The prodded and dabbed singles turned into clapped and clattered two and threes. He was twenty-seven not out and had found an accomplice in a batsman of Sri Lankan extract, known as the Mandarin who was capable of some wristy de Silvan pulls and cuts that scythed through the rocky outfield between gulley and third man where Henry lurked.

Dudley Squires was bowling, and the ball was sometimes pitching and bouncing over batsman, wicket keeper and slips, for which reason Fast Johnny had posted himself down on the boundary by the site screen. Henry realised that it was a sensible move, even if he guessed Fast's ulterior motive when he saw him reaching into his pocket for his smart phone. Then, between overs, he saw Fast sitting with his mobile attached to ear hole, and Henry shook his head as he trotted round to his fielding position.

Dudley Squires was working up a fine head steam; the boys in the slips led by Paulie Jordan were clapping him in. But Barley Reed, who now had his eye properly in, seemed undeterred and smacked a rising delivery into the ground. The ball came towards Henry and took a kick off a rugged tuft of grass and flew off in another direction... Henry had just made the fine calculation to decide that the ball was no longer quite his responsibility when he looked up. Where was Fast Johnny?

Henry scampered after the ball. As he did, he slipped and fell. Henry hauled himself up in a daze, feeling around for his John Lennon's.

They were in pieces on the ground.

He staggered towards his team mates.

"Henry, are you alright? There's blood all down your face."

"Henry, you look like the Hammer of Horror."

It was Fast Johnny, who, suddenly remembering his responsibilities to the team, had turned up from behind the sightscreen.

Henry was all ready to faint, but Fast must have sensed it and called to one of the pocket-billiarders of the squad:

"Do us a favour, Tuffers. Get him off to A & E."

Two hours later, Henry returned stoically to the fray with two stiches above his right eye.

A huge cheer went up from the French boys, who were now batting – although it would be more accurate to say collapsing as they helped themselves to the crate of beers.

Paulie Jordan was out and so, too, was Lord Sedley. The Boyling Brothers had been and gone when

Fast Johnny strode out to bat, and Henry sat down to help himself to a beer.

Paulie Jordan said:

"Just in the nick of time for the pyrotechnics."

Henry sighed and put the beer back in the crate.

"You're right," he said. "I better get padded up."

Paulie Jordan was not wrong. It was, indeed, shaping into a classic Fast innings, as Fast attempted to unleash his inner Botham. There was a four belted over long on, followed by a four belted over long off, followed by a swipe and a miss. After another swipe and a miss, followed by a beefy miscue that looked as though it was going to be caught on the boundary were it not for the fact that such an uncertain player as Feeble Dibley was underneath it.

The batsmen had crossed when Ed Valour decided – for some reason best known to his astrally challenged self - to call for a second run.

Fast, meanwhile, had pulled up at the far end with his back to Ed.

Ed was half way down the pitch, when he saw the throw bundled in second – then third bounce. He turned as if coming back down to Earth with a stone in his pocket and scampered back to the far end, but it was too late. His wicket was broken by a smug looking Constant Gardener.

Ed left the field. Wiseacres in deck chairs on the boundary edge nodded sagely at that old dictum: Never run on a mis-field, lad.

Now it was Henry's turn. He walked out for his moment of destiny – wondering whether the stiches sewn by the kind nurse whose number was in his back pocket and his nerve would hold.

"Show em a straight bat, Henry," said Fast from the other end.

Henry took guard.

By chance his first ball to be faced was from a Constant bowler known as the Whirling Dervish (on account of his unusual flaying and slaying action). Most balls from the Dervish were quite harmless. Invariably he splattered and sprayed left and right of centre (not unlike the rabble of

12

Parliament in these troubled times). But, every once in a while, he would hit his rhythm and the seam, likewise, would hit the deck.

On this occasion the Dervish delivery did just that; Henry was so taken aback as the ball spat up off length he slipped and fell back into the popping crease.

Cries of "Howzat!" went up all around him.

Henry looked up from his flattened position on the ground.

Fast Johnny was looking down at him.

"You still owe me one, Fast."

"You couldn't bet on that," said Fast Johnny without batting an eye. "A fellow who's been floored twice in one day."

The Sandpaper Affair

As a rule, I rather enjoy watching the cricket. I have always thought it a nice way to spend a summer afternoon. You can chat with friends, spice up a cucumber sandwich with a drink, and if you so choose, get merry.

The ground was situated behind the Forelock Arms where the two marquee tents had been set up. One for our team the Forelans, and the other for the Farrell's.

"Is that the last of the crates?"

"Yes, Mr. Good."

"And the glasses?"

"They're under the table, Mr. Good."

"Perfect. – Off you go and get changed then."

"Right-o, Mr. Good."

Gerald, that is Mister Good looked round at me and chuckled.

"Looks like Sandpaper's late."

"Well," I said, "that is a turn up for the books. Sandy is always a stickler for time."

The opposition Captain, Sandy was indeed late by his stickling standards. I watched as his four-wheel drive churned up the gravel and he hopped out. Sandy, I noted, was in a state of agitation that only one who knew him so well would recognise. One new pale ale had been left behind. It was all the fault of Frenchy, who forgot to remind him before they left the warehouse. And they had to go back for it, which is why they were running late and had to make the diversion. I remember as he was saying this looking around at Frenchy, who I realised must have been Sandy's new girlfriend. She was a pretty little thing in a floaty summer dress and a straw hat. She looked quite unconcerned – or so I

16

thought by Sandy's criticism. It was ever thus as far as his cricket was concerned.

Sandy looked pointedly at his watch.

"The match is due to start in fifteen," he said. "I need to go and change."

"Don't worry, Sandy," she said. "I'm sure we'll manage without you."

In all that time you may note Sandy had not said a word of greeting to me as he chucked the keys at Frenchy.

Frenchy opened up the boot.

There were several large crates (the Farrell bitter) as well as some smaller crates, including the pale ale. Ladies beers, Sandy calls them.

"Are you alright with that?" I asked.

"Of course," she said, "I put a shift in the Forelock in the old days."

"Really? – I've been going to the Forelock for years, but I don't recall ever seeing you around."

"That was before I ran away to London."

"Like Dick Whittington."

Frenchy laughed.

"More like the puss in boots."

I was amused because of the way she said it.

"Ah, there you are Cameron David!"

Sandy's lieutenant had come over to help. He was already in his make do whites. I say make do because there was always something about them that made you think he had tippexed over the grass stains.

"Hello, Cameron," I said.

"Mary," he said, "I didn't realise you were coming."

"Cameron, darling," I said, "I wouldn't have missed this mismatch for all the tea in Chipping Norton."

"Very droll, Mary."

Sandy won the toss and elected to bat.

The Forlans were still waiting for their eleventh man.

Gerald asked if they could borrow one of Sandy's men.

"I think we can stretch to that," he said. "Only you owe us a run for every minute your number eleven's late."

It was Sandy's idea of a joke, but only Cameron David laughed.

"Just teasing, Gerald. Do you know if he's actually coming?"

Mr. Good shrugged and turned to one of his teammates.

"Desmond, have you heard from Wanders?"

"He just left me a message to say he's on his way. Be here in ten according to his sat nav."

"In that case," said Sandy, "you won't give away too many runs."

"Well, Sandy," said Mister Good, "you know what I say in these situations. What goes around comes around."

Sandy could not resist it.

"I hardly think we're playing a game of rounders, Mister Good."

Then I heard, to my surprise, Frenchy say under her breath:

"God, he's such a prat."

"An extremely cunning prat."

"What do you mean?"

"You watch. He'll find a way to make them pay."

Meanwhile, Cameron David was doing that flexing thing. Bending his knees in his pads and twisting from side to side while he propped himself up by his bat. This, I suppose, was to demonstrate, vigour, keenness and general readiness for play.

"Skipper, who's umpiring?"

"I'll do it until the first wicket down. Then when we'll just play it by ear."

To explain – and sorry for those of you don't know much about cricket, Sandy always came in at number four – because he said it was the best position to bat when the shine is off the ball – and usually if a wicket went down, you could count on the ball to lose its shine by the fifth over. He always counted on umpiring through the first five overs.

"See what I mean," I said, turning to Frenchy.

"Sorry, I don't."

"Never mind. Would you care a glass of Forlan's champagne?"

"What a good idea!"

About ten minutes into the game Max Wanders turned up in a Maserati Convertible, spraying gravel all over the other parked cars, much to their owners' annoyance. He got out and strode towards the pub, calling out:

"Excuse me... I am here for the game of cricket."

This was uttered in a continental accent that had some spectators muttering into their glassware.

He was, I have to confess, a glorious sight, dressed in whites that were more appropriate to some Mediterranean night club, and noticeably tight in all the right places. In his mouth was a Gaulois cigarette and perched on the end of his nose was a pair of classic Ray-bans.

Someone said:

"You're supposed to be out on the field."

"Monsieur, I cannot possibly go out onto any field without a coffee."

A few minutes later he emerged from the pub with an expresso cup and ambled onto the field, puffing at his cigarette.

Gerald, who was behind the stumps, called to him:

"Ah, Mr. Wanders, would you mind going down to fine leg?"

Wanders stopped in his tracks and looked down at his trousers.

"They are fashion, yes?"

"Absolutely," said Gerald, smiling. "Very fashionable for cricket."

Sandy, who was standing at square leg, pointed and said:

"He means to stand over there."

"In that case," said Wanders striding up to him, "can I give you my cup?"

As he handed the cup to the speechless umpire, he tapped his cigarette onto the saucer, turned and ambled to his allotted position.

"Have you ever seen anyone look so cool on a cricket field?"

"Did you see Sandy's face?"

"It was a picture."

"Priceless - Oh, I say."

I stopped in my tracks, for Cameron David was suddenly clean bowled.

"Well, I don't suppose he could do anything about that."

"No, I don't suppose he could."

Frenchy and I watched as Sandy's lieutenant left the field. He looked utterly deflated, his bat seemingly drooping between his legs.

I could not resist:

"Hard luck, Cameron David."

Frenchy looked at me and giggled.

"You are so terribly naughty, Mary."

"I know, and so are you, darling."

At lunch the Farrell innings was still going strong. They were five men down for a hundred and twenty, and Sandy, who had entered the fray, as predicted after the fifth over, was still in. He was thirty-five not out, and I thought in a rather sprightly mood, as everyone milled around the buffet. By now, however, Frenchy, the other girls and I were all rather merry. I was having an entertaining conversation with Desmond and Gordon about the state of their property portfolios. They had invested together in a couple of houses in some part of South London I had never heard of, and it was all apparently going rather well. And rather amusingly they wanted me to invest as well. Meanwhile, Frenchy and Wanders were chit-chatting away. One could not mistake the odd light-headed chuckle from Frenchy as Wanders offered her one of his Gaulois, which must have been rather irritating for Sandy, who I knew disapproved of smoking, when I heard him say:

"You're not being very loyal."

"What's loyalty got to do with it?"

"Strange as it may seem, we are also here to promote the new ale."

"Well, I happen to prefer champers."

"It's not champers, it's English sparkling wine."

"Ah, there you are, Mary! I need some more of the Forlan's champagne."

"Of course," I said, turning around to the two Forlan players, "Desmond, Gordon! What about you two? - Would you care some of the champagne?"

"I rather think we better not."

"No, better not. Before long we'll have to go out to bat. As long as Sandy lets us."

"Mind you, I do think he's batting jolly well."

For a moment Sandy looked at them both with a rather quizzical expression. Were Gordon and Desmond being friendly or taking the Michael?

"I better go and find someone to umpire."

"Well," I said, "I am sure Cameron David will be up for it."

"You watch," I continued under my breath, "he'll be not out at the end of the innings."

Once again, Frenchy started giggling. In fact, she practically snorted up her champagne.

"Mary," she said, "you are so very naughty."

"So too, my dear, are you."

We tipped glasses and toasted Desmond and Gordon.

"Boys," I said, "we really are looking forward to seeing you bat."

As things turned out, and slightly against my predictions, Sandy got out soon after lunch – just one short of his fifty, caught with the faintest of nicks by Mr. Good behind. All, however, was not quite lost. In the last 10 overs or so there was a good sixth wicket partnership between two of the younger boys, Fergus and Finn Brownlee, who had been coaxed by their dad to play instead of two of the Farrell regulars who were otherwise though I doubt very much usefully engaged inside the Forelock. Sandpaper shook both their hands as they came off the pitch together. Finn was caught in the covers off the last ball of the innings; they had taken another fifty runs to leave the score at 190 for 7. Not a bad effort in the circumstances.

The two Nigerians, Desmond and Gordon, now came out to start the Forlan innings. For the keener observers around the ground the beauty of their technique was something to behold. They saw off the new ball comfortably, and slowly, and progressively, began to open up with shots all around the ground. Their mid-pitch chatter was highlighted by its consistency, encouragement and politeness. Desmond would say: "I say, jolly good shot." Gordon would return: "Sorry, I forgot to say wait." And Sandy would look an increasingly whiter shade of pale as the scoreboard ticked over. They just did not want to get out. The fifty was brought up, then the hundred. They were a hundred and twenty-five for nought when the Big Commotion happened.

Colin the carpenter had been minding his own business with his two spaniels as he waited his turn to bat. The dogs, although subdued by the heat, could not resist the temptation of chasing the pub cat, Smokey, who had inadvertently wandered onto the field. To be fair it would not have been much of a commotion if the dogs had not been tied – optimistically – to a couple of camping chairs. Their pursuit resulted in a trail of outdoor furniture and glasses being strewn across the outfield. Colin was mildly oblivious as he puffed on his fine Dutch tobacco. He muttered: "Oh, bugger!" and set off in pursuit of the dog and cat show.

You may have noted I am seasoned observer of Sandy, but it was only later I understood what he had done. While all this commotion was going on, Sandy ran over to the far boundary where no one was watching and where he had left his jumper with another ball hidden in it. The ball was used, but in a better condition than the one in use, with one side polished and one side scuffed up. Without getting too technical – the balance between the polished and scuffed up side enables the bowler to get unexpected and therefore surprising lateral movement – enough to confound two skilful batters such as our Gordon and Desmond.

When the dogs had been retrieved by their Master and Smokey had disappeared into the bushes, Sandy came back with his jumper and the new ball. He had decided to change the bowler, and he gave the new ball to his own faithful cocker spaniel, Cameron David.

I have been watching men's cricket a long time. In fact, you might say I have made a study of it. Their movements in the field. The way they unconsciously rub the ball against their nether regions, or more vigorously down their flanks. And Cameron David, I must admit, was one of the more vigorous rubbers of the ball.

In the space of two overs Desmond and Gordon had been removed. Caught in the slips. With Cameron David's new-found ability to swing the ball, Sandy's team begin to tear through the Forlan until they were down to Mr Good, who refused to get out as a matter of principle. Slowly the Forlans inched their way towards the Farrell score. All wickets had fallen until the last man in: Wanders. There were six runs to win and three balls left of the forty overs.

Wander's first ball whizzed past his nose. Mr Good charged down the pitch, and they managed to run a bye. Mr Good then struck the ball firmly for what he thought would be two runs, but Cameron David was lurking with a powerful throw from long off. This, unfortunately, left Wanders facing the last ball, and I could see Mr Good cursing himself at his misjudgment. He wandered down the pitch for a quick conference with the naïve batsmen.

"I'm sorry, Wanders, for leaving you with the last ball."

"That's no problem, Mr. Good. What do you want me to do?"

"In polite terms, watch the ball like a hawk and hit it as hard as you can."

Wanders nodded slowly.

"Would that be like a double handed forehand at Wimbledon?"

"Something like that," said Mr. Good, turning on his heel.

As expected, Sandy's tyro tore in and delivered what he considered to be the perfect bouncer.

At the other end Wanders performed what he considered the perfect forehand winner, striking the ball on the up and launching it over mid-wicket for six.

Much to everyone's surprise, the Forlans had won.

"Oh, my God, Wanders!" said Frenchy, grabbing him by the arm as he wandered towards the pub and the plaudits. "It might be disloyal to say this, but that was a wonderful shot!"

"You know, honestly. Mr Good is a wonderful captain. He told me to play a shot like Wimbledon."

"You played at Wimbledon?"

"As a junior. Then I found there is more to life than tennis."

Frenchy was impressed.

"Wow! You played at Wimbledon!"

At the point I thought I needed to step in before Frenchy swooned completely before the dashing Belgian.

"Well played, Max! Let's me trade you a glass of fizz for a Gaulois."

"Fair deal. I really quite like this Forlans Champagne."

"Oh, look!" cried Frenchy. "The band has arrived."

"Paco and the Snake Boots!"

"What sort of band are they?" asked Wanders.

"I have no idea," said Frenchy, looking around at me.

"Mexican folk, I think. Though, I hear they do a great cover of Thunderstruck[2]."

"Oh, please tell me it's not going to rain," said Wanders.

"Raining Men," I said.

"Oh, Mary," said Frenchy, "you are naughty!"

"So, my dear, are you!"

So, the scene settled. The sun dipping over the Cotswolds. The insects floating through its last rays. Chatter and laughter round the hog roast. The clink of glassware from the bar.

The band played a short set and then handed over to a DJ while they ate their supper. The competition

---

[2] For all those who do not know rock and roll, AC/DC are about to salute you. – Lance.

was not over as each side tried to persuade the other to drink more of their imported boissons.

"I must admit I did find rather suspicious, Desmond, when you and I were going so strong, and the ball started dipping around like a firefly on acid."

"Do you remember at Pidley when we were still batting and were required urgently in our codpieces for Rosencrantz and Guildernstern."

"You were doing Hamlet."

"No, Tom Stoppard."

"That old thesp who ran drama was a friend of his. An extraordinary gentleman. He used to act with Peggy Ashcroft and George Devine."

"How can one forget, Gordon."

"Did you go to Pidley for the drama?"

"Actually, we went on a cricket scholarship from Lagos Higher. However, we enjoyed the drama rather more. After all, in drama you can pretend to be anyone. Especially a Prince who sends emails."

"Mister Good, have you still got the match ball?"

"I think it was lost in the bushes off the last shot," said Gerald, ever the diplomat.

Without a doubt it had not been Sandy's day. Despite all his best efforts, they had been thwarted once again. To make matters worse, he had bought so much beer he was going to have to take some of it home again.

Then he saw Frenchy deep in conversation with Wanders, who had his arm draped over her cardiganed shoulder.

Spotting Gerald with the Nigerians, he sidled over.

"I say, Good. Your number eleven is being rather over familiar with my opening bat."

I could not resist:

"Has Cameron taken to wearing a dress?"

"No," said Sandy. "You know exactly who I mean."

"There's no need for a scene," said Gerald, eyeing me to come and assist.

We walked over to the offending couple.

"Wanders," said Gerald. "That was such an amazing shot. Come now, as I'm about to do the speeches."

Everyone was amused. The speeches appeared to wrap up the evening. Even though the band was still playing, people began to drift off home.

I was at the bar rolling a cigarette with Colin when I saw Frenchy leaning into someone. It was not Sandy or Wanders. It was Gerald.

I distinctly heard her say:

"I rather like this English champagne."

Gerald smiled and said:

"It's a pity we can't call it champagne. It still wins all the prizes."

"Well, it's won the prize with me. Can I trouble you for a top up?"

Sandy found me a little while later as I was enjoying the remnants of the Dutch tobacco.

"Where are they?" he said.

"Where's who?"

"Frenchy and Wanders."

"Oh, that's funny. I put Wanders into a taxi half an hour ago."

Sandy's face dropped.

"Come on," I said. "I think I should put you in a taxi, too."

"I don't want to."

"No, Sandy. It's time to call it a day."

At that moment it was hard not to feel sorry for him, although I knew better. As one of our friends was wont to say: we call him Sandpaper because anytime you deal with him, he rubs the skin off your knuckles.

As Sandy's taxi turned into the main road, I looked around.

There was still no sign of Frenchy. However, standing outside the pub, with his Gaulois and Ray-bans was Wanders.

"What did you do with Frenchy?" I asked him.

"I am not sure," he said. "I think she was a little thunderstruck."

"It must be raining men. Would you like me to put you in a taxi?"

Beware the Fruit-Cast![3]

Or why Aussies really do Crimble Crumble

[3] The scene here described is a passage of play from the 2012 Ashes test at Lords involving Shane Watson, an Australian opener and all-rounder who had the sorry reputation for regularly getting out LBW and then wasting an umpiring review; Graeme Swann, a fine, English off-spinner prone to the odd bad ball or 'filthy pie"; Chris Rogers, the most senior opener to debut in an Ashes game; Ashton Agar, the debut leg spinner and handy number eleven, having made 99 at Trent Bridge; Brad Haddin, the redoubtable keeper who all too often had to cook dinner for the Aussies on that collapsing tour. – Beef.

Now Shane is the opener, he hates to get
out,
No matter how much those Pommies
may shout,
"I'm such a great batsman, I'll stand at
my crease,
I'll hit you all over, when the ball is
released."

But in Cricket's own Eden, the Fruit of
the Plum,
Is what England were serving when
Shane came undone.
No apple, no snake, no naked temptress,
It was Shane himself who got in this
mess!

In this most luscious of orchards, Shane
planted a tree,
Right in the middle of stumps two and
three.
The Pommies? They thought he was
taking the piss,
"He's planted a big 'un, even we cannot
miss!"

He was hit there and given, reviewed and
was out,
Ego was he – and his shame all about,
Derisive laughter – Oh boy what a hoot!
"We hit your fair tree with our very own
fruit!"

Old Buck at the far end did watch in
dismay,
For Watto to blame him at the end of the
day!
Buck scanned the horizon for incoming
fare,
"Chuck your best fruit mate, I'll knock it
leg square!"

It was not a fruit that fell out of the sky,
But the pastry chef's finest, filthiest pie!
Buck could not believe it, nor could the
slips,
As the hurtling pie did strike amidships!

"Yerrout!" cried the umpire with clotted
cream haste,
And Buck started marching, no time did
he waste!
He should have stood still, should have
given the hump,
That filthiest pie was missing off stump.

The story of Shane should not end just
there,
The fruit pies were now flying
everywhere,
Young Agar came out and peered down
the ground,
To see what they all meant by "Pies flying
around!"

When he thought he had seen one, he let
out a wail,

And set off at speed: "There's a pie on my tail!"
He got down to Haddin, who returned his shout,
"No pie around here mate, go back 'fore you're OUT!"

The pie hit his stumps as young Agar ran,
It covered the wood with a sticky blue jam,
For Aussies? The lesson is really not hard,
Go read the Fruit-Cast before you take guard!

The Clout

Earl, who was also known as the Banker for reasons that will become apparent, had heard about the Clout from a scout called Dicky Bird. The Clout was on the county's books, but Dicky Bird knew personally that the Clout was not happy with his contract. "Mark my words," said Dicky. "He's a cocky sod."

"His character does not concern me," said Earl. "As long as he plays and gives it some of his clout."

Dicky laughed.

"That will all depend on what you are prepared to give as a match fee. Mark my words," said Dicky. "He knows his worth, does the Clout, and so too does his entertainer."

"You mean there is talent involved?"

Dicky threw his head back, chuckling.

"Where goes clout there is always talent," he said. "Mark my words, that one is no chit."

When they met at the hotel restaurant, it was as much as Dicky had made out.

The Clout was waiting with his frou frou in the foyer.

The Clout was a big man and stood by her chair, bat in hand, like a walking stick.

They shook hands.

The Clout turned to the clergyman's daughter. "Mr. Earl," he said, "may I present to you my fiancé, Miss Bennett?"

Earl smiled and tipped his hat.

"So this is it," said Earl. "Your mighty willow. May I see?"

The bat was in a black velvet bag, marked with the Clout's initials.

"Careful," said Miss Bennett. "He never likes to let go of it. Do you, Eddy?"

Earl picked out the bat and held it in his hand as if appraising its value in his mind. Then he took guard.

Earl began to practice a few strokes. An off drive past the despairing bowler, a cut between gulley and third slip...

"Might I inquire who made it for you? I can't imagine it was Gray, was it?"

The Clout said nothing.

"And it doesn't feel like a Nicolls..."

Miss Bennett laughed.

"He won't tell you, will you, Eddy?" she said. "It's trade secret."

"Mr. Earl," said the Clout, "now you've seen me bat, what about we get something to eat?"

The Clout ate his food as he swung his bat. With gusto. He downed his wine with equal pleasure. "I will say this, Mr. Earl," he said. "This isn't any old sack."

When the meal was over and it was time for the cigars and the port, he turned to Miss Bennett. "Betsy," he said, pointing to the cabinet particular, "Mr. Earl and I have business to discuss."

"I'll be frank with you, Mr. Earl," said the Clout as he puffed away at his cigar. "I've already had offers from the other side."

"I did not doubt it," said Earl.

"If we go on this tour, Miss Bennett comes with me."

Earl nodded and they shook hands on it.

"Let's have another drop of the port."

They did very well thank you very much over the summer. Earl was not displeased. Being a betting man, he won tidy sums against the odds, particularly in the eight-ball game.

The rules of these eight ball games were quite simple. All the normal rules of cricket applied. The batter was challenged by the bowling side to make the maximum number of runs off eight balls. The batter's partner was known as the Chump. The Chump was not a specialist batsman, but a man adept at tipping a single to get the batter back on strike. This was Earl's job. Earl was the master of tip and run. He didn't care what kind of bat was in his hand so long as he could glance or stab into the gaps.

Earl and the Clout went up and down the country challenging all the big hitters around. They never lost out once. They always found a way to beat the best that a county could put up against them.

Yet, soon enough, word got around. No one wanted to bet on the Clout. This was a problem Earl had foreseen, but he had not foreseen the Clout's reaction when he suggested the Clout use different bat just to make it interesting. "We can put it about you're prepared to play a handicap, then we'll get some good odds."

The Clout wouldn't have anything do with it.

"Either I go out with my bat, or you get a new partner."

Earl did not want to come to blows.

"In business," he said, "it is important to respect one's partner's views, which is why I suggest we cut short our season here and move onto new pastures."

Earl laid out his plan.

"I always knew you was smart, William Earl," said the Clout.

"Lizzie," he said, turning to Miss Bennett, "didn't you say you always wanted to travel to the Colonies."

Thus, they booked a passage on the steamer bound for Australia. Needless to say, Earl kept his hand in by plying his other trade on the decks.

No one wanted to play the Poms till they saw what the knuts[4] was holding. In this scheme the Clout played his part in the nets, swishing at balls and letting the Sydney Players tumble his wicket. The Clout would say things like, "Blimey, the ball comes onto the bat much quicker here." Or, "I am a proud Englishman. Or, "do you wish to knock me block off?"

This was all very humorous and taken in good jest. The Antipodeans unleashed their batsman, who was known as Hooky. Everyone swore blind this Hooky was just a rooky. Though, the Clout and Earl were not

---

[4] Edwardian slang. An idle upper-class man-about-town, and still known, according to Beefy, to frequent the streets of London. – Lance.

fooled. As it turned out, Hooky or the Hook had a rather special bat. He wasted no time hitting a four through the covers and ran a five after a cock up in the field and an overthrow. His partner, the Chump hit a single. Then Hooky hit two sixes in a row, one back over the bowler's head and the other down cow corner. A leg bye was adjudicated off his bat. In all the Antipodean made 22 runs from his eight ball.

Now it was the Clout's turn at the wicket. He hit a very flat six from his first ball, which was a full toss on leg stump. The second ball bounced outside the off and swung away outrageously. Somehow the Clout got a bat on it and sliced it over cover. The third ball was a dot ball and ran through to the wicket-keeper. The Clout was out of his crease. There was a hot dispute about this in the middle of the pitch, but the square leg umpire who had taken a shilling and some of God's willing from Earl declared him not out. The Clout had made eleven from four balls. He chipped a two through the off side. The next ball he pulled for four all along the ground. The Clout needed a six to win. The bowler let go a beamer. The Clout turned his head away and instinctively swatted at the ball. The ball flew over the boundary rope. The Clout won the loot for Earl, who had not faced a ball. But in the process the Clout's bat broke.

Earl was enjoying the victory in the arms of an Antipodean entertainer when there was a knock at the door of his hotel room.

It was Miss Elizabeth.

"Begging your pardon, it's the Clout."

"What's the trouble?"

"He's off his chump. He says he's sick."

"Well, tell him we have the return match tomorrow. I don't care if he's screwed."

"He won't get up. He says his life's over now his bat's broke."

"Well, he can pick up a new bat, can't he?"

"He says he can't. He wants the god wallah[5]. And I'm telling you that god wallah ain't speaking in Hindi.

---

[5] By which, I am reliably informed, she means a priest to comfort the bat-bereft Clout. – Lance.

He's all over the shop, and I haven't been to the haberdashers."

It was as much as Miss Bennett had made out. The Clout was totally blotto. Between them they managed to clean up the Clout and make him presentable for the challenge.

The Clout was up first. He took a great heave at the first ball and missed. All the Sydney players were chortling into their moustaches. "What's the matter, Pom? Lost your bottle." The second ball went through him again. Earl, who could see what was happening, called for the run. Since he was backing up half way down the pitch, he made it before the keeper could get his hands on the bails. Somehow the Clout had staggered up the other end. Earl, who was tall and thin, but still a fair striker of the ball, managed a four through third man, followed by a two lofted over slips. A scrambled single took their tally to eight, which "weren't" a bad effort in the circumstances.

The Australians chumped them. They made the runs in singles till the final ball which Hooky launched over the sight screen.

"I say, poor show, sir."

Earl knew they had to pay out, or they were in a nasty jar; he was already packing his bags when Miss Bennett burst into his room. She was in tears.

"Earl, he's off his onions. It's that blinking bat. Ever since it broke, he's spooked. I think he's about to croak."

"Lizzie," said Earl, "if you had any sense, you will make yourself scarce."

The clergyman's daughter now played out such a scene that Earl lost all patience. She didn't spend all this time on the graft to end up as a toe-rag in a doss house, nor was she going to jug in a dog-cart with a lot of dirty mutton chops.[6]

"Miss Bennett," said Earl, whose heart had become quite cold, as he pushed her out the door, "no one will bet on a man who has broken his bat."

---

[6] One can safely assume Miss Bennett has no desire to work for a living. – Lance.

The Boonie

(As told by L.B.W.)

Revenge, they say, is a dish best served chilled. If that is the case, our Antipodean Cousins have a peculiar way of serving it up, especially where cricket and a picnic is concerned.

Mark Hughes, known to friends and colleagues alike as Markie, had not played cricket since the under fifteens when he decided to put his name down for the clash of DPS.

Everyone said it was going to be a great day out. Among the guests were a few sporting celebrities (mainly from Aussie Rules) and retired cricketers (from the shellacked end of the Sheffield Shield).

Markie's team had won the toss and elected to bat.

They had lost several wickets; Markie was next in and feeling the tension.

To distract himself, he took one of his female colleagues for a walk along the boundary edge until they stopped behind the sight screen at the far end of the ground. Everyone else was either over by the pavilion or around the marquees.

"What's the matter, Markie?" said Maggie. "You look kind of nervous."

"Oh, it's nothing. Just a bloke's thing, I guess. I haven't picked up a bat in anger in over ten years. Even so, I can't let the boys down."

"You blokes make me laugh," said Maggie. "It's only a bloody game."

"Mags, I know you're right, but."

"Well," she said, "at least you should look presentable."

"What do you mean?"

"Tuck your shirt in."

"Trust a Sheila," he said, laughing.

"Here," she said, "let me help you."

Maggie began to laugh.

"Mags, what are you doing?"

"Honestly," she said, "why do you need a bit of plastic in your pants?"

Suddenly they heard Howzat out in the middle. Someone was out.

"Hurry, Mags," said Markie. "You better zip me up. I'm in next."

Markie stepped out from behind the sight screen and strode out to the middle, bat under arm.

He took guard and looked round him.

"Oh, no Shane! Markie's done a Boonie!"

It was one of his mates, Glen, who was standing in the slips and smirking.

The ball came towards him out of the sunlight.

Markie did not even dare lift his bat.

The ball took his middle stump.

Howzat!

The scoreboard duly noted Markie's humiliating first ball dismissal, though it failed to register Glen's off-putting ejaculation from the slips. Markie was still smarting from it as he tucked into a plate of picnic goodies when he spotted some fire ants climbing a sandwich crust near a piece of scrunched of cling film.

Markie, who was an astute observer of nature, and more particularly grass life, began to flatten out the cling film. Carefully, and with the aid of a twig, he placed the sandwich crust, along with a small core of apple, back in the cling film.

"Markie, what are you up to?"

Mags was perplexed by Markie's behaviour, as no doubt is the reader.

"Mags," said Markie, "what have you got in your bag?"

Mags began to chuckle as she emptied the contents of her bag over the picnic rug.

"Is this really part of the cricket?"

"No, Mags. But that Tiger balm of yours is just the ticket."

Markie's team were all out some time after lunch, and Glen's team were now batting. The afternoon meandered on in one of those lazy passages of play. Shots were sometimes made and wickets sometimes fell until it was Glen's turn to bat.

He strolled out to the middle and took guard; he parried the first ball and adjusted his box. He parried the second and again adjusted his box...

By the fifth ball Glen was writhing around on the pitch.

"Oh, bejesus!" He cried. "I'm on fire!"

Markie, from his position in the covers, could not resist:

"Oh, no Shane. Glen's done a boonie."

Revenge, it seemed, was a dish that could be served both hot and cold.

The Fairytale of Indore

Anika Puri was fuming. The boys didn't want to let her play.

Although she was Lakshay's sister, he didn't have the courage to argue on her behalf, so she had to sit and watch.

Rohit was quite a good bowler she thought, and Tushar could bat all day, but they really weren't that good as a group.

She wasn't about to let it drop. Her friend Myra had a little brother called Sandeep, who was small but also talented.

"Teach me to throw a ball."

"Why should I? You are a girl!"

"Because we are bigger than you. Besides, your older sister and I say so."

Sandeep was embarrassed.

57

"Why do you want to learn?"

"I really like cricket, OK? Besides, I also want to teach my brother a lesson."

So they went away and found quiet corner of the street to practice.

"See? If you throw it against the wall it bounces back, and you can catch it."

"Teach me how to catch."

She practiced every moment she could, even when it was dark.

The following week she tried again.

"Lay off it, Anika. This is a boy's game."

"Well, you're not that good at it, so does that make you a girl?"

"Go away!"

Anika waited for her moment on the side of the street.

Sure enough, the ball eventually dribbled over to her.

"Give it back!" shouted Lakshay carelessly.

The ball flew through the air and struck him in the groin.

"How did it go?" asked Sandeep.

"Now," she said, "I need you to teach me how to bat."

"If you want to learn how to bat," said Sandeep, "I'll take you to meet my friend, Rahul."

"What is so special about Rahul?"

"You'll see," said Sandeep. "He's just like that wall over there. Nothing ever gets past him."

"Howzat!"

The ball hit the two sticks they had made stumps.

Anika threw down her bat and said:

"Why can't I just hit the ball!"

"First of all," said Rahul, "you must learn to stay in."

"But I want to hit fours and sixes."

"You can't hit fours and sixes unless you stay in. You must learn to block the good balls."

"But it's so boring."

"You keep blocking," said Rahul. "Then you can hit the good balls, too. - See!"

So Anika learnt to block. She learnt to watch for the good balls, and she learnt to think of herself as a wall. She practised all day with Rahul and, sometimes, even little Sandeep.

One day, when Rahul was away playing for one of the big teams in Bangalore, Anika was playing in a street game. She was batting and doing very nicely blocking the ball. No one could get her out, and the bowler, who was one of the big boys, was getting annoyed.

"Anyway," said Kapil for that what his name, "why should girls play in our games?"

"If you don't want me to play in your game," said Anika, "you must get me out."

"But all you do is block the ball."

"I can't practise my shots if I get out."

"Girls should play for girls' teams."

"What's the best girls' team?"

"Haha, the Pashmeekers!"

"Do you know anyone there?"

"I don't care about girls' teams."

"Well, if you don't care about girls' teams, you better get used to me batting."

Kapil bowled her a Yorker, but Anika dug it out easily. He bounced her, and she swayed out of the way, laughing:

"Is that the way to treat a lady?"

It began to get dark.

Kapil, who wanted to go home to his mummy and tea, said:

"We have to go soon."

"But you haven't got me out. Do I get to keep the ball, too?"

"You are very irritating," said Kapil, or something much worse in Malwi[7].

"Tell you what," said Anika, "I'll retire on one condition."

"Girls can't give conditions."

Anika frowned and took a guard.

"Give me your best ball, big man."

Kapil began to taunt her, wiggling his hips and cooing at her as if she was a Bollywood star.

"Alright!" he said. "You asked for it."

Kapil bowled the ball.

Anika blocked it dead and picked the ball up.

"See you tomorrow," she said, walking off.

"Where are you going with our ball?"

"The Pashmeekers. Maybe they can get me out."

---

[7] A dialect of Hindi, spoken in the city of Indore, which Mary once entered on an elephant. – Beef.

Gentlemen, Players and

Chokers

(A naughty homage to E. W. Hornung[8])

Raffles was playing a game at Lord's for the Gentlemen of Essex when he was approached, at

---

[8] E.W. Hornung (1866 – 1921) was an English author best known for writing the A.J. Raffles series of stories about a gentleman thief and amateur cricketer in nineteenth century London. – Mary also adds he was married to Constance, Arthur Conan Doyle's sister, and was a good friend of naughty boy, Oscar Wilde. - Beef.

the lunch table, by a young cricketer by the name of Crowley.

Like everyone else, Crowley was dressed in creamy whites, but Raffles noted at his neck a cravat with a light blue and pink stripe that could only be described as in rather poor taste; besides which his jumper bore not the crest of Rose but her inferior cousin, Wait.

"Say what, Raffles," he gushed. "That is a fair delivery you have up your sleeve. I don't reckon that beanpole had a clue what he was up to."

Raffles recalled the delivery that had got through the defence of the gangly Essex opener who swiped haplessly, and in retrospect, at his Chinaman before sloping off chump-like, but he merely smiled.

"I don't know what you are up to on the weekend of the 4th, next month," went on the young man. "But we're looking for cricketers to come and play for my twenty-first. My father, Lord Sedley asked me to put the word out."

"Your father is Lord Sedley, owner of Downton Abbey?"

"The very fellow. – You will come down, won't you?"

"The weekend of the 4th you say?"

"Dougie Mountjoy is coming down from the Sticks. And we may have even got Fenwick Cooper to roll his arm."

Raffles pretended to think about it over lunch, which was a rather liquid beef stew followed by an extremely sticky toffee pudding. He put in another good spell after lunch and took their number four's off stump with a wrong un that went straight. They got the men of Wessex all out for under one fifty. He came in at his usual position, just over half way down the order, and was able, with the aid of young Crowley, who was gamely holding up the other end, to hit the winning runs – a dashing, one bounce four over the bowler's head. Amid the gushings of Crowley and the back slapping of his team mates, Raffles felt there was no other game quite like cricket. At least he had not found one that afforded him these moments of cool satisfaction; apart from the unmentionables, of course, but he kept those thoughts even from his innermost self.

"Crowley," he said, "about that game of yours on the fourth, I rather think you have persuaded me. I must keep this form while it holds. Besides, the country air is always so good for the skins."

"Raffles, I am so glad you can come. I will advise my dealer of your requirements."

"However," said Raffles, "I do have one favour to ask of you. I will need to bring my understudy, Bunny Hamilton."

"Hamilton," said Crowley, nonplussed. "Is he a player?"

"Why," said Raffles, "Bunny Hamilton may not yet be known on the Tavern Stand, but his cover drive is coming along nicely for a gentleman."

All of which was news to Bunny himself. "Raffles," he cried, "you know I am utterly hopeless at cricket. In fact, cricket is all croquet to me."

"Relax, Bunny," said Raffles. "No one is going to put you through the hoop. Besides, I'll make sure you field behind the wicket."

"But I've never stood at slips."

"I mean, by the sight screen, you chump... Gaffer Steward rarely – if ever misses the ball. He has the safest pair of hands in the county."

"Be that as it may, Raffles, I can't hold a bat. I barely know middle from leg."

"Bunny, I am not asking you to get spicy here. Besides, we will have plenty of time to practice."

He asked Bunny to fetch his pick locks from the secret compartment in the desk drawer.

"What is your game, Raffles?" asked his companion, still confused.

"Bunny," said Raffles, laying out the pick locks upon the table. "One can never be certain of the game. However, I fully intend to take advantage of Lord Sedley's hospitality. Tomorrow we start in the park with your back lift."

There were two nets in the local park, rarely used, except by the odd school dasher and turbaned wrist spinner. But Raffles was unperturbed – focusing on six-yard throw-downs (Raffles disdained continental metrics). In the context Bunny was developing a decent forward defence, but he had too much bottom hand in his follow through, which made him - Raffles averred - vulnerable to a catch in the covers, even if his timing was often so awry that Raffles was not sure it would reach even the keenest of poachers. Bunny was often despairing and Raffles disparaging by turns. It was a minor miracle they managed to make it down to Dorset without falling out, but that was due, as ever, to Bunny's general amenability and bonhomie as they set off on a well-nigh perfect morning for motoring.

The sun accompanied them along one of Hampshire's discreet roads. (Raffles disdained the motorway on the reasonable grounds that he never liked to risk a copper's speed gun.) only to be marred by a few droopy clouds as they wafted over the county line into Dorset. Raffles hastily pulled up the roof of the Jag. There was a trickle of rain on the windscreen. Bunny, who was warming himself under a blanket, felt they deserved a break at the wayside inn. Raffles did not disagree.

Entering the establishment, Bunny strode over to the bar to order their bitters and lemons; only to have Raffles grabbing his arm.

"We need to leg it."

"I say, Raffles," said Bunny, snatching the packet of salt and vinegars that he had in all decency purchased from the frosty looking barman. "What's going on?"

But Raffles said nothing, and they walked back out. Bunny could not fail to notice the customer sitting behind the door. She was what could only be described as one of those ambidextrous types in a lounge suit. There was a smirk on her face and a trace of tash Bunny was bound to recall upon reflection, reminding him, incongruously, of the artist, Tacita Dean and a bowl of rosewood patchouli.

"Come on, Bunny," said Raffles. "I just remembered there's a better place up the road."

He could not deny it. Bunny felt an utter chump as he sat down to dinner in the Downton dining hall. The Sedley coat of arms was proudly emblazoned on the oak panelling. Various Tudor and Elizabethan ladies and gents glowered from the walls. Eighteenth century hunting parties brandished muskets as if dropping titbits for their hounds.

They were a party of twenty-four: chaps in cummerbunds and smoking jackets, girls in little black numbers, ladies sagging in the vales of silicon.

Bunny was overwhelmed by the prestige of Lord Sedley's party, while Raffles mingled easily with the minor stars of silk and screen, the odd hack and BBC broadcaster. He was sat next to Saffy, who turned out to be the rector's daughter and Bunny thought the only normal person in the room until he realised she was more than just a little drunk, and also an itsy bit high.

Saffy kept dropping her napkin and bending to inspect the legs of the table.

On the third occasion Bunny bent down with her and they bumped noses.

"Oh, I say," said Bunny.

"I'll forgive you," said Saffy, "as long as you promise to kiss it better."

It was an awkward moment, and Bunny was thankful when Lord Sedley rose to his feet to welcome his guests and propose a toast.

There followed a rather painful speech. Lord Sedley attempted to explain *le regle du jour*, according to Duckworth Lewis. It was all getting rather confusing, especially as Saffy kept on making comments behind her hand.

"I'm not supposed to say anything," said Saffy behind-handily. "but entre nous, there is a Scotland Yard detective in our midst."

"You're joking."

"I am not. Apparently, there are two well-known thieves in the area."

Bunny was suddenly horrified, recalling Raffles' strange behaviour at the inn, and the strange type in the trouser suit with the reedy moustache.

"Really," said Bunny, "what could they possibly get from this lot of munchkins?"

"Just look at that pearler," said Saffy. "It must be worth more than the proverbial China in a cabinet of curios."

Saffy pointed to the necklace that one guest, Lady Gaga, was wearing. Bunny scrutinised the lady at the end of the table, sitting beside Lord Sedley, and concluded, even if her jewels glistened in the candelabra, she did look rather addled.

"Surely, they won't get away with it with all these bodyguards around?" said Bunny.

"Bodyguards? – What are you talking about?"

Bunny pointed to a well-built young man in a purple suit sporting an ear-ring.

"That's Lady Gaga's PA, you chump."

"Does he bat?"

"Not here, as far as I know. Besides, he's from Paris."

"Anyway," said Saffy, "I'm just glad these little hoops are fake."

"They look pretty convincing to me."

"Do you think so?"

"Mind you, they are not as pretty as your lobes."

During pudding (there was a choice of Eton Mess and Gateau) Saffy had gone off to speak to one of her girlfriends, and Bunny had to endure the company of a Scottish photographer named Cellphone. Or so Bunny thought. Which, no doubt, explained his rather feeble joke about the Scotsman's web address. But the

Scottish photographer was not one to appreciate feeble jokes, even when they were accompanied by inane chortles. After a while, Bunny began to doubt his professionalism; Cellphone spent most of his time taking selfies with the other guests.

Bunny was dying to have a word with Raffles about the smirker in the pub earlier that day. But there was no opportunity until the Taylors and the Havanas had been and gone, and they were ensconced back in their rooms.

Bunny relayed the news Saffy had related to him and how he was sure it was the female detective at the inn, but it turned out, Raffles had already been informed by Crowley. Moreover, the detective was actually Cellphone, really a disguised Inspector Dalglish.

"Dalglish, you mean that celebrity detective."

"The very same. As for your lady at the inn, she is not a detective, but a infamous thief. In fact, the leader of the gang Dalglish is after."

"Really, Raffles, is that possible?"

"Just because she's wearing a suit, does not mean to say she does not know how to pick a lock, or use her front."

Raffles now began to pace the room; Bunny watched him.

"Bunny," declared Raffles upon the second turn. "You don't know what an opportunity this gives us. If we play our cards right…"

"I don't know about the cards, what about the run of the ball? At some point tomorrow I'm going to have to bat." said Bunny, who was feeling rather more circumspect.

"Honestly, Bunny. I'm not talking about the cricket. I am talking about the chortler round that gaga woman's neck. And, besides, you will be fine as long as you remember to bend your arm as you were taught."

"Raffles, I've only had a couple of throw-downs in the park on a Sunday morning. I hardly think that is going to equip me to face a Sedley beamer."

"It slips out of his hand. You just have to watch it and duck."

"Be that as it may, Raffles, you promise you won't take any risks."

"Bunny, a cricketer must always take risk into calculations. If not, we would block ourselves into oblivion.

And there's nothing more dispiriting than a forty-ball duck, especially if you have a wager on your reputation."

"What are you talking about?"

"I bet Fast Johnny I would come away with the Gaga chortler."

The weekend continued normally. Bunny began to enjoy himself. On the cricket field, a lucky, running catch early on assured him his pride, which swelled at a smiling wave from Saffy on the boundary edge.

"I can't wait to see you bat!" she cried. "I bet you'll really knock them out. Or even for six!"

As it turned out, Bunny did. When faced with the Sedley beamer, he stepped away to leg and scooped it over the slips in a manner – the cordon concurred - Jos Buttler would have been proud of. It was only a shame the next delivery was a Yorker from out of the Cathedral that upended both Bunny and his stumps.

Raffles, who was playing on Lord Sedley's team, helped Bunny to his feet.

"Hard luck, Bunny. There was not very much you could have done about that."

Bunny was asleep and dreaming of scooped sixes and switch hits in a scintillating partnership with Raffles when he was woken by a noise outside his room.

He opened the door and found Inspector Dalglish struggling with Saffy.

"Take that, you pig."

Saffy launched a slap at the erstwhile photographer.

"I caught him taking a photo while I was asleep, the perv."

"She's lying. I caught her sneaking into Lady Gaga's room."

"Mr. Hamilton, please hold the slapper."

"Bloody cheek! I am not a slapper!"

"Hold her, Mr. Hamilton!"

Dalglish ran downstairs, while Saffy remained in Bunny's clutches.

He soon realised it was other way round.

"Are you going to give me a kiss now, Bunny?"

Bunny went bright red.

Saffy laughed and said:

"In that case, I better give you one."

Bunny did as he was told and stood with his eyes closed.

When he opened them again, Saffy had vanished.

Crowley and Lord Sedley were standing in their silk pyjamas, followed by Lady Gaga's French assistant in a purple jumpsuit and sleeping goggles.

"Madame Gaga's window is wide open. La boîte de la chocker is been derobée. Madame is out for the conte."

"She has a count in her room?"

"No, Monsieurs, she is been drugged."

"What's going on, Bunny?" said Raffles, who now appeared in his dressing gown at the top of the stairs.

They rushed into Lady Gaga's room. The window was wide open, and her necklace box, as the Frenchman averred, was gone from its place on the top of the dresser.

"Confound it!" said Lord Sedley. "What is going on, Raffles?"

Suddenly, there was a cry from downstairs.

"It's the inspector!" cried Raffles, taking command of the situation. "Quick, everyone! We must help him."

"Coming, Raffles!" cried Lord Sedley, stumbling over Crowley and Bunny in his eagerness to get the bottom of the stairs.

There was Daglish with Saffy in a most inelegant half nelson.

"Got her at last!" he said. "Where is the chortler?"

"I haven't got it."

"Don't lie."

"I'm not lying! I was merely interested in Lady Gaga, not her pearls."

It was a sorry state of affairs, but both gentlemen and players agreed to shake hands on it. Match abandoned due to theft was recorded in the scorebook.

Raffles and Bunny took advantage of the fine motoring weather to return to London.

"Bunny, why don't you drive?"

"Are you sure, Raffles? I would hate to damage the car."

"You'll be fine. I just need a kip."

"Don't tell me, Raffles, you were also having a rendezvous with Lady Gaga last night?"

"Bunny," said Raffles, pulling a familiar box out of his pocket, "I am *chocked* that you should think such a thing."

Charcoal Special

(As told by S.W.)

If revenge is a dish best served chilled, then surely self-righteousness is a dish best not served at all.

Most went deep into Mrs. Digby's vegetable patch. Some became stuck on the roof of the Forelock Arms. And some again ended up in the greenhouse of a nearby cottage.

"And I'm not giving it you back!" shouted Mr. Gibbs as he picked the cricket ball up underneath the broken window.

"It's not his fault," said Stephen the glazier, who had come to put the putty in the following day. "Finn Brownlee just loves his batting."

"I am sorry, but I couldn't care less. Nobody said anything about the cricket club when we bought the bloody house. All these cricket balls are really beginning to nark me off."

"How many do you actually have?"

"Fifteen so far."

"Seriously? – Why haven't you thrown them away?"

"If I'm honest, I hate waste."

"Will you let me have a look?"

In a corner of the greenhouse was a grotty, old chest of drawers, much soiled and cobwebbed.

Mr. Gibbs tugged at the bottom drawer.

"Wow!" said Stephen, picking out one of the used balls. "That one there is the charcoal special."

"The charcoal what?"

"They are quite a rarity."

"How do you know about them?"

"Followed the game for years. Though, I don't play myself."

"I don't understand how you could watch it! As far as I'm concerned, it's a total waste of a Sunday."

"Thought you Saffers were almost obsessed with the cricket as you were with rugger."

"Don't get me started on the rugby. It's never been the same since they introduced quotas."

"Tell you what," said Stephen, brightening. "I can recycle these balls for you if you want."

"As long as they go to a good home. Like I said, I hate waste."

Stephen finished puttying in the window and handed Mr. Gibbs the bill.

He glanced at it and said:

"Rest assured, I'll be sending this on to the Brownlees. By rights, they are the one who should be paying it."

Stephen was in the Forelock Arms that night where Mr. Good was drinking at the bar with John Brownlee and Colin.

"Stephen," he said, "haven't seen you for a while. Fancy turning out for us on Sunday?"

"Thanks, Gerald. It's not for me, as you know."

He sipped his beer.

"Can I interest you in a supply of slightly used cricket balls?"

"That would be good," said the captain of the Forlan Team, turning to his drinking companion. "Don't you agree, John? We always need more net balls."

"Finn will be over the moon I am sure," said John Brownlee.

Mr. Gibbs was relaxing with a Gilroy's Serious in his conservatory when the ball crashed through the window.

"I don't bloody believe it."

As he picked up the ball, a sense of familiarity came over him.

"You complete utter bastard. This time it's going on the braai[9]."

---

[9] South African for barbecue. Much like their test team when they tour. – Lance.
Haha, mate! The English team can limbo under anything. – Beef.

The Tailender's Scorecard

It was two o'clock in the morning; everything was going swimmingly when Henry turned around and saw Ed Valour swaying on the barstool beside him.

"Could kill one of those gin slims you're drinking only I appear to be short of a bob or two."

Henry giggled and felt in his pocket:

"Ed, never you mind. It looks like I've been left in charge of the plastic."

"The missus would be onto me like a double shot if she knew I got me hands on the plastic. By the way," said Ed, "what has happened to Fast Johnny?"

"Search me, Ed, search me. - Looks like he's gone home to the good lady."

"The masochist. I thought she kicked him out."

"I have it on good authority," said Henry. "She always takes back him again around about now."

"Henry, are you alright, mate?"

Finally, Ed twigged when he looked down and saw the plastic on the counter.

They both started giggling hysterically as the barman came to take their orders.

"Doubles all round!"

Just as the statement pertaining to a piece of plastic can never lie, nor can the score-card: all out for thirteen, scrawled across the page along with several tee-heeing emojis that had been placed there by the thirteen-year old squib recruited on a tub of vanilla and chocolate ice cream.

The match in question took place between the Occam Arms and our old friends, the French House. Needless to say, conventional wisdom has it that the failure of the French House to make their score passingly competitive was down to the introduction into the attack of Tim Sims, their ageing, crock-kneed but nonetheless cunning leggie. But this, upon reflection, was not the reason for the French Boy's abject failure, which resulted being awarded the Tailender's Scorecard at the end of the 2018 season.

The night before half the team had been out on a spectacular binge instigated and organised by Fast Johnny upon the streets of Soho. - It seemed an American distribution company had bought Fast's crackling Story of the Spitfire, replete with images and theme tune of Kenneth More's Douglas Bader reaching for the skies. He was now convinced – as indeed were Henry and Ed at 4 o'clock in the morning staggering out of some dodgy club where several student do-gooders in fancy dress cavorted to "You're the One I Want" the Yanks would now buy his company. Fast Johnny could retire with a small fortune– according to some quirk of Ed's addled brain – of copper coils laid for China.

When the French Boys arrived on the field of play, in their customary dribs and drabs, and painfully beyond the fashionably late, the old timers who had denied themselves the revels merely shook their heads. Besides, it was a glorious day. The sun was out in Oxfordshire, and they knew they were going to get a very nice tea and crumpet courtesy of their hosts.

It had been a hot summer. The Occam pitch was looking somewhat baked. Groggy-eyed they went out to inspect it. There were cracks all over the place. In fact, it was demonstrably one of those uncovered pitches so enamoured of certain cussed ex-cricketers and Yorkshire commentators. It was agreed that no fast balls would be bowled, and that everyone would be bowling off their short runs. (As Henry said, Fast Johnny did not count, since he always bowled off a short run.)

The French boys – by some sleight of hand which had Fast grubbing around in the grass for the trusty five cents piece kept for such purposes in his wallet – won the toss and duly, and to the relief of their sore heads, elected to bat. Henry and Lord Sedley went out to face the chinless music.

Henry ran out Lord Sedley when endeavouring to scamper a single under the influence of the Alka Seltzer fizz guzzled from Paulie Jordan's water bottle.

The French boys were already nought for one when, in the second over, Henry swiped pathetically at Tim Sim's looping leg break and spooned the ball to slips. From there on things went progressively downhill.

The Boyling Brothers normally so reliable in crisis were in a hurry to get home – they had been on the go all the long weekend – and were due on Monday to help out on Chef's farm. Both got out slogging: Billy to a caught and bowled, no score. Brian caught on the boundary for a single as the batsmen crossed the second time. Will Deedes and Paulie Jordan threatened to take the score into double figures, but they too were underdone by the unusual bounce generated off the Occam's baked Alaska. Fast Johnny top scored with four, one of those typical Fast one bounce launches over the bowler's head. Ed Valour, forever the only stoned man in the party, remained two not out.

The boys slumped down at a table outside the Occam Arms. The only question remained for Henry – now on his third wind due to the Alka Selzer - who was going to buy his rounds?

Henry was looking around pointedly at Fast Johnny as he said this. Fast, who was hooked to his mobile madly texting his bookie, barely looked up.

"By rights," he said, "as the team top scorer you should be honouring me."

"Don't be ridiculous," scoffed Henry. "That was merely your bog standard scoffing score. By rights, you should be scoffing up for us, Fast."

Ed smirked through tombstone eyes.

"Off you go, Henry."

"Yes, Henry. And while you're at it -."

Henry feigned a wounded expression and shuffled off to the bar.

"I can't believe we were all out for twelve," said Paulie Jordan, suddenly sunk by the whole depressing nature of their efforts. "I mean, that was on the scale of an England batting collapse."

"You're right, Paulie," said Lord Sedley. "Some people would say there was match fixing going on."

"Tell that to Tim Sims. He's going to frame that ball on his mantlepiece."

"I don't know about framing the ball. He'll want that pitch with him for the rest of the season. And the seasons to come."

"Well, that settles it," said Fast, acknowledging the pint placed before him. "Either I'm up fifty or I'm quids in, or I've blown the lot on the 4.10."

"In that case," said Henry, as he sat down with his beer and reached in his pocket, "you'll need this."

He threw the plastic down on the table.

Fast Johnny looked at him without batting an eyelid and said:

"That's the one that's been batting for the Spitfire."

"If only it had been batting for us!"

"Well, it is now," said Henry, raising his glass.

63 Not Out[10]

For cricket fans how sad the news
The felling of poor Phillip Hughes
Full blooded swipe at short pitched ball
Endless courage says it all.

Neither bowler nor headgear's fault
But ill luck's strike like lightning bolt
If only you'd the chance once more?
Another heave! The crowd would roar!

Talent you had for sure in spades,
With dext'rous hands and flashing blade,
As you reflect from heaven above
You left whilst doing what you love.

Life is short and from all we've seen,
If you'd stayed, what might have been?
On sporting stage there's no encore
Better leave them wanting more!

---

[10] Cricket is the sadder without the fearless Aussie
left-hand batter, Phillip Joel Hughes (1988 – 2014).
RIP also Colin Bateman: bowler, batter, carpenter
and dog owner. Go well on the cloudy Oval, mate. –
Lance and Beef.

The Sandpaper Affair
First published in Great Britain by

Leopard Publishing Ventures Ltd
Hampshire SO212PR
www.magickgate.com
Instagram: magickgatebooks

ISBN: 9780957455092

ACKNOWLEDGEMENTS

The cover image has been derived from a Cassell's magazine illustration by John H. Bacon of E.W. Hornburg's short story, 'Gentlemen and Players' (1898) in the public domain. Hornburg's original story can be found in *Raffles: The Amateur Cracksman* (1899), available as an e-book from the Gutenberg Press. The illustrations that accompany each story are from Punch's *Story of Sport* (1910), now in the public domain.

M.T. Sands Interview

(As Told to Kurt Brown)

- "I always had such a wonderful time in the bazaars. You know I once hid in a carpet shop."

- "Darling, I merely record. I don't judge or criticise. It's so ghastly when everyone starts wagging their fingers. And shouting each other down. I must say, I don't like all that shouty writing that's telling you what to think or do. We have to make up our minds about that ourselves, don't we?"

- "Sometimes one has to do what one has to do, especially to take one's mind off one's predicament."

We talk to MT Sands about her life on the road, her love of the bazaar; her writings and affairs, but not her diet or beauty tips.

We meet in Belton House of the Braceless Country Estate, Lincolnshire – very kindly made available by her new boyfriend, the horse-mad Sheik, Ali Al-Buti. "No relation to the terror family," I am told as I am ushered into the Nineteenth Century Salon. "He's been so terribly sweet but rather shy and retiring on a Saturday morning. Would you care for something to drink? – A cup of tea. Lapsang Souchong. Gunpowder Tea, there's bergamot in it, hits you like the charge of the light brigades. If you prefer coffee, there's instant, or Sainsbury's own brand espresso."

All this comes tumbling out before I have time to scribble in my notebook. "You're not taping me. Don't tell me you are one of those gentlemen of the press who still knows how to do short-hand. I always wanted to learn, though I have to content myself with the phonetic alphabet and the schwa. You do know the schwa," she says. "It's everywhere in the English language."

M.T. Sands ers at me and rolls her eyes. Then, as if this is still part of the joke, feigns death throes.

"What about that drink?"

"I think I'll just have a glass of water," I say.

"Still or sparkling."

"From the tap is fine."

M.T Sands jumps up and leaves the room. She returns with my glass of water a few moments later, as I am contemplating what appears to be an oil painting of the sheik in riding boots and jodhpurs – half naked from the waist up to reveal a rather prominent nipple piercing.

"You've got one of the bee glasses," she says. "And I've got one of the hives. Don't you think they're lovely?"

I smile; she smiles back.

And I glance down at my notebook.

M.T. Sands is now leaning back on the sofa, one leg tucked under her – and one flip flop dangling off her big toe (she appears to be inspecting the chipped varnish of her big toe). The sofa is a conventional sofa but extends like a divan. It is draped with throws – rather lovely Clarice Cliff looking things, surrounded by peacock feathers. It is all rather light and airy in the room. And perhaps for this reason, or the fact that I suddenly become aware of the smiling Cupid upon the commode behind her that the notebook slips from my lap.

As if anticipating a clumsy child, M.T. Sands leaps to her feet and pushes the notebook back before it slips further.

I thank her and once again we resituate.

"In the resume that you so kindly sent us you allude to your various adventures and misadventures."

She laughs.

"There have been rather a lot of those, which is why I wrote the book of stories."

"Of course."

She pauses – almost as if to inspect the silence and then tumbles on.

"Have you ever been to Arabia? - I had such a wonderful time in the bazaars. It's a much better way to shop, don't you think? – Why do we need supermarkets, or hypermarkets for that matter? It is the most boring to shop unless of course you are in Waitrose in Winchester, which I am not, very often. But that wasn't what I was thinking."

"What were you thinking?"

"Not thinking. Rather reading about Lady Ellenborough and her Bedouin Prince. Lady Ellenborough was one of those great Victorian adventuresses, and besides which an amazing horsewoman. And her Bedouin prince was in awe of her. As were the Damascenes during the Druze and Maronite crisis... She must have had them around her little finger. They called her sheikha mother of milk. Rather charming, don't you think?"

"Anyway, you were telling me about your misadventures in the bazaars."

"I was?"

I nod and M.T. Sands laughs.

"Soon you'll be putting words into my mouth."

"I'll try not to."

"Of course, if you want a misadventure, there was the time my Italian boyfriend, Riccardo, who liked to think he was a count, though I was never too sure, even if he did appear to have a crumbling tower in Calabria or somewhere. He chased me through the bazaar and that's the time I ended up hiding in the carpet shop."

"Why ever did you do that?"

"I would have thought it's quite obvious. He was getting rather jealous. Sexual jealousy is such a terrible emotion, don't you think? We are here for such a short time. It seems so ridiculous to get uptight about it all."

"I suppose," I say, choosing to take her at her word, "it depends on the circumstances."

"Oh, rot to the circumstances. It's all about character. And sometimes one just needs a bed for the night. People these days are far too worried about offending their own characters. At least Riccardo made no bones about his jealousy... Do you mind if I smoke? They are not real cigarettes. They're fakes ones. From time to time I like to hold them. Would you like one, too?"

I shake my head.

She lights up one of her fake cigarettes and inhales.

"I am quite partial to the odd cigar."

She takes another puff, followed by a pause, which seems to lend space to her racing thoughts.

"Some of them were really awful you know, dribbling one-eyed monsters. But their stories often made up for it."

"Anyway," she says finally, "what's wrong with being a little naughty?"

"It says here -"

I begin to read from the resume that is printed on pink paper (defined when it was handed to me as the Beardsley i.e. naughty pink.)

M.T. Sands begins to chuckle.

"I'm sorry," she says, "but I do think it's rather good, don't you?"

"Elsewhere, I think was in last month's *Tatler*, I've heard you claim to have no career."

"I am sure that's right. I made a career of having no career. The Sheik says it's my Wildean streak, but I am not sure if a woman can have one of those these days. Are you sure you are okay with your tap water? There's a rather good whisky in the Sheik's drink's cabinet, an Oban."

I decline the whisky and try to persist with my line of questioning:

"So, you write for the sake of writing."

"No, I listen for the sake of listening. And sleeping. I write afterwards."

"I thought you just didn't think of it like a career."

"Now you are putting words into my mouth. Of course, I am serious about what I do."

M. T. Sands looks at me with the stars still twinkling in her eyes.

"And I was absolutely serious when I said I made an art of having no career. As a teacher, I worked and travelled all over the world, but I began to feel like an absolute fraud. And this is the truth with teaching, one always reaches a point with it when one feels like a fraud. I mean, really people, if they feel so inclined – and that includes little children – and all good teachers know this, teach themselves. In this sense teachers are like writers. They are only as good as their students, and writers are only as good as their readers. But I digress."

"You do?"

"I thought we were puffing my book."

"Indeed, what do you have to say about your book?"

At which she throws back her head - in the process launching the flip flop that has been dangling from her big toe across the room – and laughs:

"The Sheik says it's a spanking good read."

Ten Naughty Stories

By M T Sands

"A luminous bit of prose delicately piled on prose platters"

Jay Parini

M.T. Sands grew up in southern England. She ran away from school when she was sixteen and lost her virtue in a field in Burgundy, under the vines of Clos de Tart, to a mystical and long-haired young German who claimed to be able to divine the kabbalah from a rather weathered notebook which had H. H. inscribed in fading, gold leaf on the cover. For several days she followed him on her bicycle until she ate some Pierre che Rire cheese and realized she was being an absolute fool. Thereafter her career began.

The Half Days

By Sedley Proctor

Ex-pat adventure in Southern Italy

Young, English teacher, Julia arrives in a vibrant Southern Italian city where she takes up with happy-go-lucky street seller, Cofi. When Cofi is caught up in a smuggling ring, the question of her own future arises. But as the half days stretch into the summer nights, the future is forgotten in a round of carnival pleasures.

Accidental Death

Of a Terrorist

By Sedley Proctor

Crime passionnel in Southern Italy

What reasons can there be beyond the reasons of love? Now married to successful businessman, Achille Lombardo, Julia appears to have it all until her she embarks on an ill-fated affair with Arturo, and her ex-pat adventure morphs into the crime of passion.

The Junk Book

By Sedley Proctor

High and Dry in Nineties London

Was it the junk that made him creep? Or some scratching at his itchy soul? No matter, there was no solution other than to trigger the gun. - On the brink of fame and fortune, Jimmy Quentin, poet maudit of the Q-tips, leaves his wife, Suzy high and dry and takes to the streets where his life continues to spiral out of control.

***

It was a matter of some urgency: a wolf was loose in the woods. And being loose in the woods, he could get into the garden.

"Whatever you do," said Dad. "Don't go out the gate. You don't want the wolf to eat you."

Laila went out the door, but the wolf was already in the garden.

"There you are!" he cried. "I was wondering where you got to."

"What are you doing here?" she cried. "This is my garden."

"Well," said the wolf, "you're not in your garden. You're in my garden now."

***

The Wolf Garden

By F. M. Frites

A Totally, Completely and Utterly Bodacious Adventure with Unicorns and Gnomes

Dreamy tomboy, Laila meets Cyril, a rebellious gnome and passes through a charmed gate into the Wolf Garden. Here, she does battle with the shape-shifter Smarm and his army of wolves. When Smarm captures her gnome friends and steals the magic strawbs, Laila and Cyril help the Mistress Dido win them back.